SCIENCE PROJECT IDEAS

Science Project Ideas About

THE MOON

Robert Gardner

Enslow Publishers, Inc.

44 Fadem Road   PO Box 38
Box 699   Aldershot
Springfield, NJ 07081   Hants GU12 6BP
USA   UK

Library of Congress Cataloging-in-Publication Data

Gardner, Robert, 1929–
    Science project ideas about the moon / Robert Gardner.
        p. cm.— (Science project ideas)
    Includes bibliographical references and index.
    Summary: Introduces the phases and other characteristics of the moon through a series of experiments, most of which can be used to start a science fair project.
    ISBN 0-89490-844-8
    1. Moon—Experiments—Juvenile literature. 2. Science projects—Juvenile literature. 3. Science—Exhibitions—Juvenile literature. [1. Moon—Experiments. 2. Experiments. 3. Science projects.] I. Title. II. Series: Gardner, Robert, 1929– Science project ideas.
    QB582.G37 1997
    523.3' 078—dc21
                                  97-6486
                                      CIP
                                      AC

Printed in the United States of America

10 9 8 7 6 5 4 3 2 1

Illustration Credits: Jacob Katari

Cover Photo: Jerry McCrea

☆ CONTENTS ☆

☆ INTRODUCTION ☆

In this book you will find experiments about the moon. The experiments use simple everyday materials you can find at home or at school.

The book will help you to work the way real scientists do. You will be answering questions by doing experiments to understand basic scientific principles.

Most of the experiments provide a lot of guidance. But some of them will raise questions and ask you to make up your own experiments to answer them. This is the kind of experiment that could be a particularly good start for a science fair project. Such experiments are marked with an asterisk (*).

Please note: **If an experiment uses anything that has a potential for danger, you will be asked to work with an adult.** *Please do so! The purpose of this teamwork is to prevent you from getting hurt.*

Science Project Ideas About the Moon *can open science's door to you—and draw you out into the mysterious light of the moon!*

MEASUREMENT ABBREVIATIONS			
centimeter	cm	meter	m
foot	ft	mile	mi
inch	in	miles per hour	mph
kilogram	kg	miles per second	mi/sec
kilometer	km	pound	lb
kilometers per hour	kph	second	sec
kilometers per second	km/sec		

The stars about the lovely moon hide their shining forms when it lights up the earth at its fullest.

(Sappho)

1

OUR NEIGHBOR: THE MOON

The moon is our closest natural neighbor in the sky. It revolves around the earth as our only natural satellite. There are many other much smaller satellites going around (orbiting) the earth, but they were put there by humans.

The moon appears to be about the same size as the sun, but it is really much smaller. It looks as big as the sun because it is much closer to us than the sun is. The sun is approximately 150 million kilometers (94 million miles) from the earth. The moon is only about 384 thousand kilometers (239 thousand miles) away. Because the moon is so close to us, its diameter (width), which is 3,480 km (2,160 mi), appears to be as big as the sun's diameter. But, in fact, the sun's diameter (1,400,000 km, or 870,000 mi) is almost exactly 400 times as big as the moon's and 109 times as big as the earth's. In Chapter 3 you will see how the distance to the moon can be measured. And in Experiment 3.2, you will measure the moon's diameter for yourself.

The moon's distance from the earth changes because its orbit (its path around the earth) is not a perfect circle. Its orbit has an oval shape called an ellipse. When the moon is closest to the earth, we say it is at perigee. When the moon is at perigee, it is 356,000 km (223,000 mi) from the earth. When the moon is farthest from the earth, we say it is at apogee. When the moon is at apogee, it is 407,000 km (254,000 mi) from the earth. Because the moon's distance from the earth does not change very much, its size seems to be almost constant. However, as you will learn in Chapter 2, its shape appears to change quite dramatically.

On the earth's surface, the average temperature is 20°C (68°F). Temperatures above 58°C (136°F) or below -89°C (-129°F) have never been recorded. On the moon, temperatures change much more. The moon has no atmosphere and relatively little water to absorb heat. Until recently, it was believed that there was no water on the moon. However, data from a satellite that orbited the moon in 1994 indicate there may be a shaded reservoir of ice near the moon's south pole. Because so little heat is absorbed by the moon, temperatures in lunar darkness fall to -170°C (-274°F), well below the temperature of dry ice (solid carbon dioxide). (We sometimes use the word lunar to describe things that are related to the moon. It comes from the Latin word for "moon," *luna*.) In direct sunlight, lunar temperatures can reach 134°C (274°F)—well above the temperature at which water boils. Even though the moon's interior is much cooler than the earth's, experiments show that the moon, like the earth, is still radiating heat into space.

The earth has more than 80 times as much mass (matter) as the moon. As a result, the force of gravity on the moon is much less than it is on the earth. Someone who weighs 45 kg (100 lbs) on the earth would weigh only 7 kg

(16 lbs) on the moon. That is why astronauts find it so easy to walk on the moon. But because the force of the moon's gravity is so small, it cannot prevent gases from escaping its surface. Lacking gases, the moon has no atmosphere.

The moon's average speed around the earth is 3,680 kph or 2,287 mph. It completes one orbit in just about 27.3 days. But the time between one full moon and the next is 29.5 days. Why does it take two days longer to go from one full moon to the next than it does for the moon to make one orbit around the earth?

The reason is that while the moon makes one orbit around the earth, the earth moves along about one twelfth of its orbit around the sun. Consequently, the moon has to travel a little more than one full "circle" before it is again in line with the earth and the sun (see Figure 1).

Like the earth's crust, the moon's most abundant element is oxygen. Of course, the oxygen does not exist as a gas, because the moon has no atmosphere. Oxygen on the moon is chemically joined to many other elements. Silicon, too, is abundant on the moon; so are calcium, aluminum, and magnesium. Unlike the earth, the moon contains very little hydrogen. This is because the moon has little

FIGURE 1

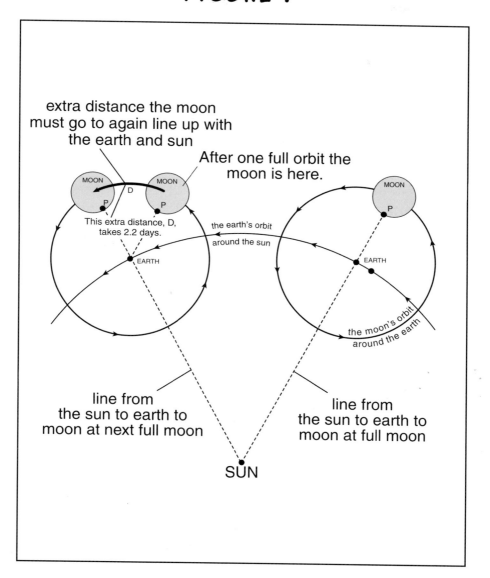

The moon makes a full orbit around the earth in about **27.3** days. However, since the earth orbits the sun, the time from one full moon to the next is **29.5** days. The moon has to travel an extra distance (**D**) to make a point (**P**) on the moon (that directly faces the earth) again line up with the earth and sun to create a full moon.

water, which is one-eighth hydrogen by weight.

The earth has a molten (liquid) iron core. The movement of the electric charges in the liquid produces a strong magnetic field. The earth's magnetic field makes it possible for us to use a compass to navigate. The moon may have an iron-rich core, but it has no magnetic field. The information scientists have gathered about moonquakes shows that the moon is rigid throughout. This solid moon has no fluid to carry electric charges. Therefore, it has no magnetic field. (In Experiment 1.1, you can see for yourself that moving charges produce a magnetic field.)

Two thirds of the moon's surface is made up of highlands that are rugged like mountains. The highlands reflect a lot of light because they are made up of light-colored rocks that contain calcium and aluminum. The smooth, lower portions of the moon are covered by darker rocks that contain a lot of magnesium, iron, and titanium. These rocks and dirt reflect less light, so we see those areas as the darker regions of the moon. When humans first looked at the moon through telescopes, they thought the dark areas were seas. They called them *maria,* the Latin word for "sea," and we still call the dark areas maria today.

Many geologists believe the moon was originally very hot. About 3.5 billion years ago, it had cooled enough to form a thin, solid crust. At that time it was hit by a number of large meteoroids that broke through the new surface. The magma beneath the crust then welled up, flooding the lowlands with lava.

The back side of the moon—the side we never see—has no maria. Its entire surface is very light. Scientists believe that the crust on the far side of the moon had become so thick that the meteoroids could not break through it. As a result, lava did not flood the lowlands on the back side of the moon.

Actually, we do see a little more than half the moon. The moon wobbles slightly as it revolves around the earth. Over time, its wobbling allows us to see almost three fifths of its surface.

Both the mountains and the maria of the moon are covered with depressions, called craters. The craters were made by meteoroids (pieces of matter flying through space). Since the moon has no atmosphere, any meteoroid headed for the moon will hit its surface and produce a crater. Most meteoroids that approach the earth burn up as they pass through our oxygen-rich atmosphere. The streak of light that marks a meteoroid's path in the sky is called a meteor. Meteors are often called shooting stars. But they are not stars. They are actually chunks of rock moving through space that happen to enter the earth's atmosphere. They glow with light because they are burning. If any part of a meteoroid reaches the earth's surface, it is called a meteorite.

DID YOU KNOW. . .?

It is believed that about 65 million years ago a huge meteorite, probably an asteroid, struck the earth. The impact was so great that it created an enormous dust cloud that blocked out much of the sun's light. The reduced light caused the earth to cool, killing many plants. Because of the cooler temperature and less food (plants) to eat, dinosaurs could no longer survive and became extinct at this time.

Experiment *1.1

MOVING CHARGES AND MAGNETIC FIELDS

To do this experiment you will need:

- ✔ an ADULT
- ✔ long piece (several feet) of insulated copper wire
- ✔ magnetic compass
- ✔ flashlight battery (D-cell)
- ✔ wire stripper or knife
- ✔ clear plastic tape

It is believed that the moon does not have a liquid core because scientists have found it has no magnetic field. Because the earth has a liquid core, electric charge can move inside the earth. Moving charges give rise to magnetic fields.

To see that moving charges produce a magnetic field, you will need a magnetic compass, a long piece of insulated copper wire, a flashlight battery (D-cell), some clear plastic tape, and **AN ADULT** to help you.

If the ends of the insulated wire are not bare, **ASK AN ADULT** to use a wire stripper or a knife to remove about an inch of insulation from each end of the wire. Use pieces of clear plastic tape to hold the middle

FIGURE 2

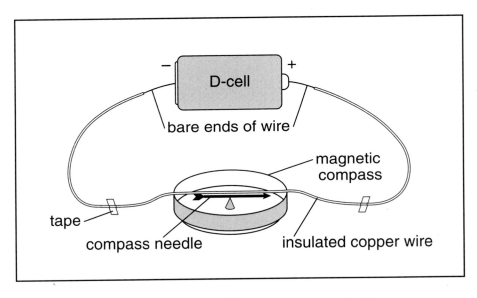

Moving charges produce a magnetic field.

region of the long wire on top of the compass. The wire should be parallel to the compass needle, as shown in Figure 2. Touch the ends of the wire to opposite ends of the D-cell. When you do this, electric charge can flow through the wire from one end of the battery to the other. What happens to the compass needle when the charges move? What changes if you turn the D-cell around? What changes if you put the wire under instead of on top of the compass?

Questions About the Moon

 Here are some questions about the moon. How many of them can you answer and be sure you are right?

(*Can you see the moon every night if it is clear?*

(*Can you ever see the moon in the daytime?*

(*Is the moon in the same place every night at the same time? If your answer is no, will the moon be east or west of the place you saw it last night at the same time?*

(*Why does the shape of the moon appear to change?*

(*Does the moon always rise in the same place on the horizon?*

After you do the experiments in this book, you will be able to answer all these questions about the moon, and many more as well.

O, swear not by the moon, the
inconstant moon,
That monthly changes her circled orb.

(William Shakespeare)

2

WATCHING FOR THE MOON

You can learn a lot about the moon by just watching it and its place in the sky. Keep a notebook to record your observations about the moon. Look for the moon as often as you can. Each time you see it, note its place in the sky and its distance from the sun and make a drawing of what it looks like. Experiment 2.1 will help you to find the moon.

Experiment *2.1

WATCHING THE MOON DAY BY DAY AND NIGHT BY NIGHT

To do this experiment you will need:

- ✔ daily newspaper with information about the moon
- ✔ notebook
- ✔ pen or pencil

Daily newspapers have information about the moon, which is usually printed in the weather section. Use the newspaper to find the date on which a new moon occurs. Several days after the date of a new moon, look for the moon as the sun sets.

It is perfectly safe to look at the moon as much as you want, but **NEVER LOOK DIRECTLY AT THE SUN. IT CAN CAUSE SERIOUS DAMAGE TO YOUR EYES!**

What does the moon look like as the sun sets? Draw a picture of it. Where is it in the sky (in what direction)? Which side of the moon, the side closer to the sun or the side farther from the sun, is brighter?

How far is the moon from the sun? Before you try to answer this question, read the next section on measuring things in the sky.

Measuring Things in the Sky

Distances in the sky are usually measured as angles. Sometimes the sun and moon appear close together. They might be less than 10 degrees apart because they lie almost on the same imaginary line extending from your eye into space.

FIGURE 3

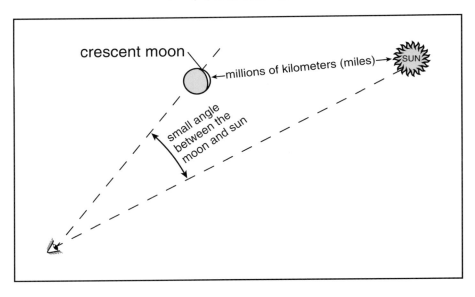

Even though the sun and moon may appear close together in the sky, they are really millions of kilometers (miles) apart. They appear to be close when the angle we see between them is small.

Actually, they are about 150 million kilometers (94 million miles) apart. The moon is much closer to the earth than the sun (see Figure 3). Stars are even farther away than the sun. When people say a star is close to the moon, they mean that the angle in the sky between the moon and the star is small.

If you hold your fist toward the sky at arm's length as shown in Figure 4a, it will cover approximately 10 degrees in the sky. To see that each fist really is equal to about 10 degrees, start with one fist closed and extended toward the horizon. Go fist-on-fist upward as shown in Figure 4b, until one arm points straight up. You will find it takes just about nine fists to reach this point. Since from horizontal to straight up is 90 degrees, each fist must cover about 10 degrees (9 x 10 degrees = 90 degrees).

Measuring the Separation of Moon and Sun at Sunset

To find the distance between the sun and the moon at sunset, cover the sun with one hand as you begin (see Figure 5). **NEVER LOOK DIRECTLY AT THE SUN. IT CAN CAUSE SERIOUS DAMAGE TO YOUR EYES!** Then find how many fists separate the sun and moon. Record

FIGURE **4**

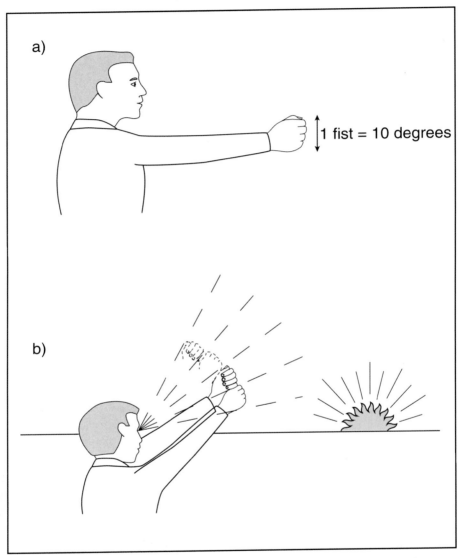

a)

1 fist = 10 degrees

b)

a) One fist at arm's length covers about 10 degrees in the sky.

b) You can see that this is true by going fist-on-fist upward from the horizon. You will find it takes nine fists to reach an overhead position.

FIGURE 5

Cover the sun with one hand as you begin to measure the distance (angle), in fists, between the sun and moon.

the number of fists separating them in a notebook, along with the date and time. Where is the moon in the sky? That is, in what direction do you have to look to see it? Is it in the west, southwest, northwest, south, east, or some other direction? How many fists is it above the horizon? (The angle of the moon above the horizon is its altitude in the sky.) What happens to the moon after the sun sets? Does it follow the sun? Does it move east or west in the sky?

FIGURE 6

Date	Time	Moon's Direction	Angle Between Sun and Moon	Moon's Altitiude	Direction of Moon's Motion	How the Moon Looks
12/6	4:45 P.M.	SW	2 Fists	3 Fists	E to W	

This chart shows the beginning of a record to keep track of the moon over time.

In your notebook record the date, time, location of the moon in the sky, number of fists between the sun and moon, the moon's altitude, direction the moon moves, and any other information you think might be useful. Your first record might look like the one in Figure 6.

Try to observe the moon at about the time of sunset each clear evening for the next few days. Make the same measurements you made before and record them in your notebook. What happens to the shape of the moon during these days? What happens to the distance (number of fists) between the moon and sun from one day to the next? What happens to the moon's location in the sky at sunset as the days pass? Is the moon moving more to the east or to the west of the sun as days go by? What does this tell you about the time that the moon rises? Is it rising earlier or later each day?

Finding the Moon Before Sunset

During the days that you are observing the moon at sunset, try to find it earlier in the day. Can you see the moon in the daytime? If you can see it, where is it in the sky? Record any observations in your notebook.

See if you can find the moon shortly after it rises. Where (in what direction) would you expect to see it rise? At about what time would you expect to see it rise?

Finding the Moon After Sunset

After you have seen a full moon at sunset, can you see the moon at sunset on the next night? on the night after that? Can you find the moon after sunset on these nights? If you can, when does it set? What happens to the moon's setting time as days pass? What has happened to the moon's shape?

Approximately how many fists does the moon move in one hour? How could you estimate the distance (angle) between the sun and moon even if the sun has set?

Finding the Moon in the Morning

After you can no longer see the moon at sunset, begin looking for it early in the morning, before, during, and after sunrise. What has happened to the moon's shape? How far is it from the sun? Is it east or west of the sun? Which side of the moon (left or right) is now the brighter side? Is this the side nearer to or farther from the sun?

As the days pass, does the moon move closer to or farther from the sun? What does this tell you about the moon's rising time? What happens to its shape as the days pass?

Finding the Moon Over Longer Times

Continue your observations of the moon for several months. You will begin to see a pattern to the moon's motion and changing appearance. How much time passes between one full moon and the next?

During your continuing observations, look to see where the full moon rises on the horizon.

Experiment *2.2

DOES A FULL MOON ALWAYS RISE AND SET IN THE SAME PLACE?

To do this experiment you will need:

- ✔ daily newspaper with information about the moon
- ✔ chalk
- ✔ notebook
- ✔ pen or pencil
- ✔ magnetic compass

From your newspaper, you can find the exact day when the moon is full. Watch for the rising full moon over the course of a year. Choose a point where you can clearly see the moon rise. Use a piece of chalk to mark the point where you stand to watch the moon rise. If possible, choose the same point to watch the moon set. Stand in that same place each time you watch the moon rise or set. In a notebook, record the position that you see the moon on the horizon as it rises. In the same notebook, record the place where you see the moon set on the horizon. Your record for the first day of this experiment might look like the one in the following example. You might also record the time of moonrise and moonset as well.

——————————⋆⟨⋆————————————

Date	Me	Moonrise	Me	Moonset
Sept. 10	At center of driveway (X marks the spot)	Just left of big oak in Mr. Brown's yard	At center of driveway (X marks the spot)	Directly over Mrs. Lee's garage

To make a rough estimate of the moon's direction when it rises and sets, hold a compass at the place or places where you watched the moon rise and set. Be sure to hold the compass away from metals such as a belt buckle. Position the compass so that the compass needle points in a northerly direction. (It is not likely to point to true north. That is, it probably will not point exactly toward the North Pole, which lies almost directly beneath the North Star.) In what general direction did the moon rise? In what general direction did the moon set?

Repeat this experiment at full moon each month for at least a year. Always stand in the same place to watch each moonrise and each moonset. Does the moon rise in the same place on the horizon every month? Does the moon set at the same place on the horizon every month?

At what time of the year does the moon rise in the southeast and set in the southwest? At what time of the year does the moon rise in the northeast and set in the northwest?

The Harvest Moon

 The time when the sun is directly above the earth's equator is called an equinox. There are two equinoxes each year. The vernal (spring) equinox occurs on or about March 20; the autumnal (fall) equinox occurs on or about September 20. The full moon that occurs closest to the fall equinox is called the harvest moon. It is called the harvest moon because the moon rises shortly before or after sunset for several days around the time of the full moon. As a result, farmers have more light than usual in the early evenings to harvest their crops before frost and cold weather set in.

Experiment 2.3

TIMING THE HARVEST MOON

To do this experiment you will need:

- ✔ calendar or almanac
- ✔ daily newspaper with information about the moon
- ✔ clock or watch
- ✔ notebook
- ✔ pen or pencil

Use a calendar or almanac to find the date of the fall equinox. Then find the date of the full moon that is closest to the equinox. What is that full moon called? Check your daily newspaper to find the time of sunset and moonrise for several days before and after the full moon. Use a clock or a watch of your own to find the time of sunset and moonrise as you see it. How do your measurements compare with those in the newspaper? Can you explain why they might not be exactly the same?

Normally, the moon rises about fifty minutes later each day. How much later does the moon rise each night during the three days before and after the harvest moon?

The first full moon after the harvest moon is called the hunter's moon. Does the moon show a similar rising-time pattern around the time of the hunter's moon?

What do you think the rising-time pattern of the moon would be around the spring (vernal) equinox? Use an almanac to check your prediction. Were you right?

DID YOU KNOW. . .?

In the southern hemisphere, the harvest moon occurs after the spring (vernal) equinox. The hunter's moon occurs about a month later in late April or early May.

*Everyone is a moon, and has a dark side
which he never shows to anybody.*

(Mark Twain)

3

MODELS OF THE MOON AND EARTH

From your experiments in Chapter 2, you know that the moon's shape always appears to be changing. Its rising time and its setting time also change every day. The place on the horizon where the moon rises changes from day to day. So does the place where it sets. The side of the moon closest to the sun is always brighter than the side farthest from the sun. The bright part of the moon gets bigger as the moon moves farther from the sun in the sky. The bright part of the moon gets smaller as the moon and sun move closer together in the sky. If you see the moon in the morning after sunrise, the left side is the brighter side. If you see the moon in the evening after sunset, the right side is usually brighter.

To try to explain why nature behaves as it does, people suggest ideas, called theories. These theories are often called models. Sometimes models made of real things are used to illustrate the ideas. In this chapter, you will test a model that illustrates why the moon appears to change the way it does.

Experiment *3.1

A MODEL OF THE MOON, EARTH, AND SUN

To do this experiment you will need:

- ✔ dark room
- ✔ lamp with bright lightbulb
- ✔ partner
- ✔ light-colored ball, about 5–10 cm (2–4 in) in diameter, mounted on a stick (a Styrofoam ball works well)
- ✔ clay

To make this model of the moon, earth, and sun, you will need a dark room. Turn on a lamp with a single bright lightbulb at one end of the room. Have a partner stand beside you holding a Styrofoam ball or another light-colored ball mounted on a stick. If the ball is made of Styrofoam, the stick can be pushed into the ball. If the ball is solid, use some clay to mount it on the stick. Have your partner stand to your left while you face the light, as shown in Figure 7.

In this model, the light represents the sun. Your head represents the earth. The light-colored ball represents the moon. Since you

FIGURE 7

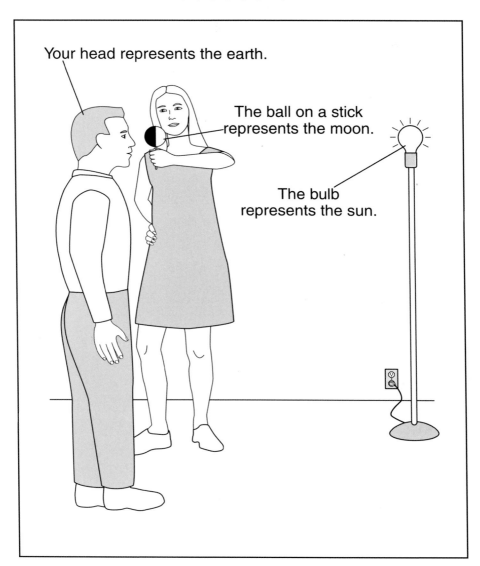

Your head represents the earth.

The ball on a stick represents the moon.

The bulb represents the sun.

A model of the earth, moon, and sun shows how the moon's appearance changes over time.

are facing the light, the model now represents the earth at noon, when the sun is in the middle of its path across the sky. The moon (the ball in this model) is to the east. Slowly turn your head and body toward the east (counterclockwise, toward the moon). Your turning represents the earth as it rotates on its axis. You see the moon rise in your model. After making one quarter of a turn, the sun (lightbulb) will be on your right (west). It is now a setting sun. The moon is directly in front of you, so it is in the middle of the sky.

Figure 8a shows the earth (your head), moon (ball), and sun (lightbulb) in your model from above. You (the earth) are facing the moon after one quarter of a turn. Half the moon you see is bright; the other half is dark. Have you ever seen the moon when it looked like this? If you have, was the sun setting or near its setting time when the moon was in the middle of the southern sky?

Now continue to turn slowly to your left to represent the rotating earth. You will see the moon set after another quarter turn. As you continue to turn, you will see the sun rise and move slowly across the sky. Then you will again face the moon.

In this model, the moon moves slowly around the earth. After a week (seven full

FIGURE 8

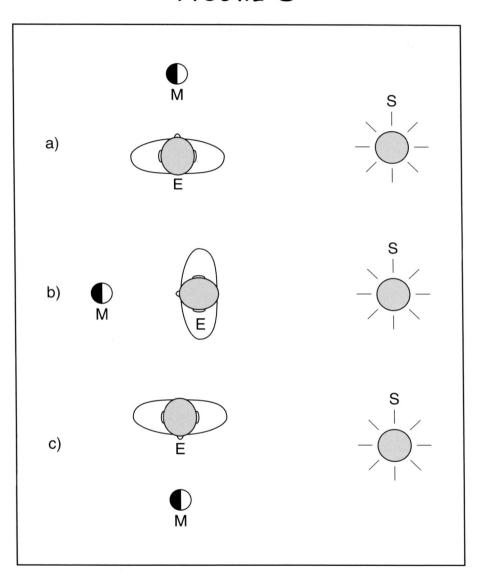

This model of the earth (E), moon (M), and sun (S) uses your head for the earth, a lightbulb for the sun, and a ball for the moon at: a) first quarter; b) full moon; c) third quarter.

turns of the earth) the moon will have moved to a point where it is on the opposite side of the earth from the sun. To represent this model, have your partner slowly move the moon (ball) one quarter of the way around you while you make seven complete rotations (turns). Your partner should also slowly turn the stick so that the same side of the moon always faces the earth. Watch what happens to the moon's appearance as you make these turns. When you face the moon now, as shown in Figure 8b, it will be a full moon. (If the moon lies in the shadow of your head, have your partner raise the stick to lift it above your shadow.)

During another seven turns of the earth (your head), the moon will move slowly to the position shown in Figure 8c. At this point, again only half the moon you see is bright. But it is now the other half that receives the "sunshine." After another seven turns of the earth, the moon will lie between the earth and the sun. Since no reflected light can reach you, you will not see the moon. It is a new moon. Of course, a room is not a perfect model of space. Some light reflected by the walls and ceiling will reach the ball. This makes the dimly-lighted ball visible. In the space around the real moon, there are no walls or ceilings to reflect light.

Repeat the experiment once more. While you (the earth) turn about 28 times, have your partner move the moon once around you. Then give your partner a chance to be the earth while you move the moon slowly about the earth.

About the Model

 A good model will agree with what is found in the real world. So let's consider how well the model you tested agrees with what you have seen in the real world. For any one day (one full turn of your head), did the moon look pretty much the same?

Over the course of a month (one full circle of the ball around you), you saw the moon's (ball's) appearance change. Did these changes match the way you saw the real moon change in the sky? That is, did it go from a thin crescent to a half-moon, to a full moon, to another half-moon (with the opposite side bright), to another crescent (but reversed), and then dark (new moon) as it passed between the earth (your head) and the sun (lightbulb)?

If your answers to these questions are all yes, and they probably are, then the model of the moon is a good one. The model shows that as the earth rotates on its axis, the moon moves around the earth about once each month.

Figure 9 is a diagram of the actual model. It shows the moon orbiting (going around) the earth as the earth orbits the sun. The actual time between new moons (when the moon passes between the earth and the sun) is 29.5 days. Since all the months except February have 30 or 31 days, there can be two full moons in one month. When this rare event happens, the second full moon is called a blue moon.

Look at your calendar. Will there be a blue moon this month? this year? What do people mean when they say "Once in a blue moon"?

The Distance to the Moon

One way to measure the distance to the moon is to aim a radar or laser beam at the moon. The beam will reflect off the moon and return to the earth. By measuring the time between the moment the beam is sent and the moment it returns, the distance to the moon can be calculated. It can be calculated because we know that radar and laser beams both travel at the speed of light, which is 300,000 km/sec (186,000 mi/sec). It takes about 2.6 seconds for the beam to travel to the moon and back. The total distance the laser light or radar beam travels is 780,000 km (484,000 mi). (This is because 300,000 km/sec times 2.6 sec equals 780,000 km.) But, the

FIGURE 9

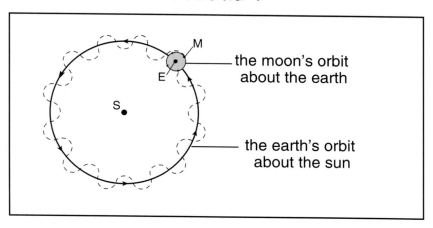

the moon's orbit
about the earth

the earth's orbit
about the sun

The actual model is one in which the moon orbits the earth as the earth orbits the sun. The path of the moon as seen from the sun is shown by the dotted line. (The diagram is not to scale.)

beam has traveled to the moon and back. We must therefore divide by 2, making the distance to the moon 390,000 km (242,000 mi).

Careful measurements show that the moon's distance from the earth changes. At its closest point to the earth, a point known as perigee, it is about 356,000 km (221,000 mi) from the earth. When the moon is farthest from the earth, we say it is at apogee. When the moon is at apogee, it is 407,000 km (253,000 mi) from the earth. Because the moon's distance from the earth does not change very much, its size seems to be almost constant. However, its shape changes a lot, as you have seen.

Experiment *3.2

THE SIZE OF THE MOON

To do this experiment you will need:

- ✔ pencil
- ✔ ruler
- ✔ file card
- ✔ scissors
- ✔ meterstick or yardstick
- ✔ clay

Knowing the distance to the moon makes it easy to find its size. Use a pencil and a ruler to draw a square 0.6 cm (0.25 in) long and wide near the center of a file card. Cut out the square with scissors. Use a small piece of clay to mount the file card near the end of a meterstick or yardstick, as shown in Figure 10a. Hold one end of the meterstick or yardstick close to one eye. Turn the other end toward the moon. Start with the card far from your eye so that the moon fits inside the square. Slowly move the card toward your eye along the stick until the moon just fits inside the square, as shown in Figure 10b. The length of the square now matches the diameter (width) of the moon.

FIGURE 10

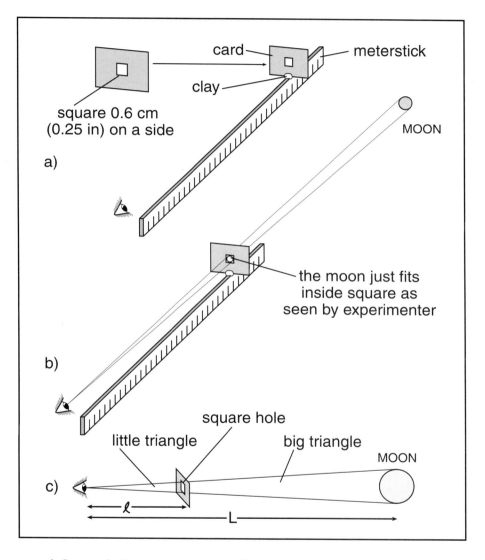

a) Cut a 0.6-cm square in a file card. Mount the card on a meterstick.

b) Move the card until the moon just fits inside the square hole.

c) The little triangle from your eye to the square is part of the big triangle from your eye to the moon. Therefore, ℓ ÷ 0.6 cm = L ÷ diameter of the moon.

As you can see from Figure 10c, the little triangle between your eye and the square in the file card is a part of the big triangle between your eye and the moon. As a result, the length of the little triangle divided by its base (0.6 cm, or 0.25 in) will equal the distance to the moon divided by the moon's diameter. You can find the length of the little triangle divided by its base. It is the distance from the end of the stick (where your eye was) to the file card divided by the length of the square hole (0.6 cm, or 0.25 in). For example, if the card was 72 cm (30 in) from the end where your eye was, then that length divided by 0.6 cm (0.25 in) is:

72 cm ÷ 0.6 cm = 120,

or 30 in ÷ 0.25 in = 120

As you can see, the result is the same whether you use centimeters or inches. This tells us that the length of the big triangle (390,000 km, or 242,000 mi) divided by its base (the moon's diameter) is also 120. If the distance to the moon is 120 times its diameter, then dividing its distance by 120 should give us its diameter:

390,000 km ÷ 120 = 3,250 km,

or 242,000 mi ÷ 120 = 2,017 mi

What is the diameter of the moon according to your measurements?

Experiment *3.3

A SCALE MODEL OF THE EARTH AND MOON

To do this experiment you will need:

- ✔ 2 Styrofoam or other soft, opaque spheres: one 5 cm (2 in) in diameter, another 1.3 cm (0.5 in) in diameter
- ✔ stick 1.5 m (60 in, or 5 ft) long
- ✔ 2 toothpicks
- ✔ tape
- ✔ sunlight
- ✔ a friend

The model you used in Experiment 3.1 explained the changes that the moon goes through every month, but it was not to scale. That is, it was not based on the actual diameters of the earth, moon, and sun or on the distances between these objects.

To make a scale model of a house, you might build a model in which each one-meter length of the house was represented by one centimeter in the model. If the house were 10 m wide and 15 m long, the model would be 10 cm wide and 15 cm long, as shown in Figure 11.

To make a scale model of the earth and moon, you can use what you have learned

FIGURE *11*

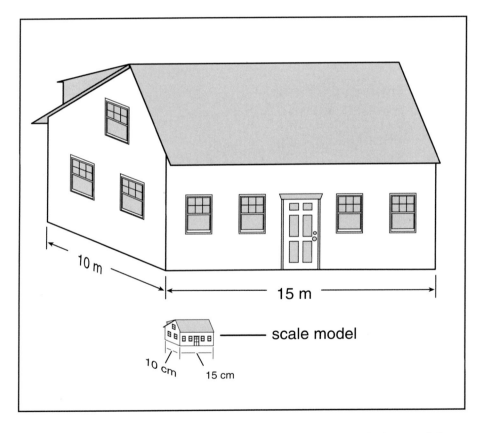

10 m

15 m

scale model

10 cm   15 cm

In this scale model of a house, one centimeter of the model represents one meter (100 cm) of the actual house. The scale, therefore, is 1:100.

about the moon and what you know about the earth. The information you will need is given in Table 1. How does the number in the table for the diameter of the moon compare with the value you found?

TABLE 1

INFORMATION NEEDED TO MAKE A SCALE
MODEL OF THE EARTH AND MOON

UNITS	DIAMETER OF MOON	DIAMETER OF EARTH	DISTANCE BETWEEN THE EARTH AND MOON
KM	3,480	12,800	390,000
MI	2,160	8,000	242,000

As you can see, the earth's diameter is almost four times larger than the moon's, because 12,800 km ÷ 3,480 km = 3.7. The distance from the earth to the moon is about 30 times the earth's diameter (390,000 km ÷ 12,800 km = 30.5). To make a scale model of the earth and the moon, use a Styrofoam ball with a diameter of 1.3 cm (0.5 in) to represent the moon. To represent the earth, use another Styrofoam ball with a diameter about four times as big. One with a diameter of about 5 cm (2 in) will do nicely. You will also need a stick 1.5 m (150 cm) or 5 ft (60 in) long and two toothpicks. Tape the toothpicks to opposite

FIGURE 12

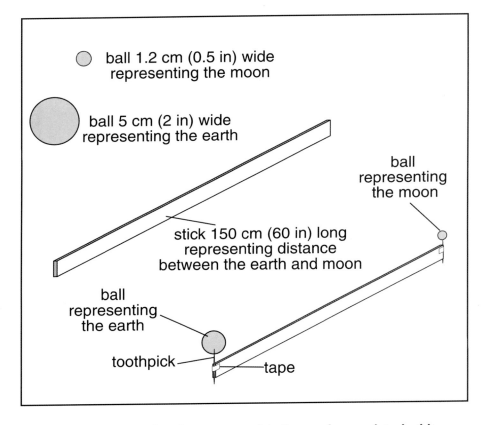

ball 1.2 cm (0.5 in) wide
representing the moon

ball 5 cm (2 in) wide
representing the earth

ball
representing
the moon

stick 150 cm (60 in) long
representing distance
between the earth and moon

ball
representing
the earth

toothpick

tape

A long stick, toothpicks, tape, and balls can be used to build a
scale model of the earth, the moon, and their separation.

ends of the stick and push the balls onto the sticks, as shown in Figure 12. Remember, the larger ball represents the earth, the smaller ball represents the moon. The diameters were chosen so that the earth's diameter (5 cm, or 2 in) is about four times the moon's diameter (1.3 cm, or 0.5 in). By choosing the balls' diameters in this way, we have a scale model of the earth and the moon. Since the earth and the moon are about 30 earth diameters apart, the length of the stick should be 30 x 5 cm = 150 cm (60 in) long. In that way, the separation of the earth and the moon in the model will be to the same scale. (If you prefer, you can reduce the scale by half and use a stick 75 cm [30 in] long and spheres that are 2.5 cm [1 in] and 0.6 cm [0.25 in] in diameter.)

It would be nice to include the sun in this model. However, the sun's diameter is more than 100 times the earth's diameter. You would need a lightbulb more than 5 m (16 ft) wide! Worse yet, the sun is more than 10,000 earth diameters away. To keep the same scale, you would have to place the 5-m-wide lightbulb representing the sun 500 m (almost 1/3 mi) away from the ball representing the earth.

Since a scale model that includes the sun is not practical, you can use the real sun. It is

FIGURE 13

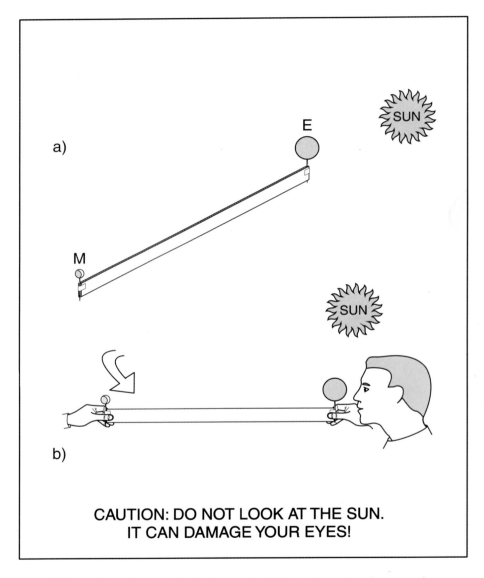

CAUTION: DO NOT LOOK AT THE SUN.
IT CAN DAMAGE YOUR EYES!

a) Hold the stick so that the earth (E) is closer to the sun than the moon (M).

b) Have a friend slowly turn the stick around you as you watch the moon (M) from the earth (E).

very much out of scale for the rest of the model, but it is the best you can do for now. Hold the stick so that the earth is closer to the sun, as shown in Figure 13a. Place your eye near the ball that represents the earth. Have a friend slowly turn the other end of the stick around you, as shown in Figure 13b. Remember, **NEVER LOOK AT THE SUN! IT CAN DAMAGE YOUR EYES!** Can you see the different shapes (phases) of the moon that you saw in the earlier model?

Using your scale model, you can make an eclipse of the moon. Tip and turn the stick until the sun, earth (larger ball), and moon (smaller ball) are in line. When they are, the earth's shadow will fall on the moon. By turning the stick slightly, you can see the moon move into and out of the earth's shadow.

If you look closely, you can see that the earth's shadow on the moon is curved. It was the actual earth's curved shadow on the moon that led early Greek astronomers to believe that the earth had the shape of a sphere (ball).

Experiment *3.4

ANOTHER SCALE MODEL OF THE EARTH AND MOON

To do this experiment you will need:

- ✔ globe (with a stand)
- ✔ ball with a diameter of approximately one-quarter the diameter of the globe
- ✔ scissors
- ✔ meterstick or yardstick
- ✔ string
- ✔ sunlight on an open field
- ✔ a partner
- ✔ tape
- ✔ early-morning or late-afternoon sun

A larger scale model of the earth and moon can be made using a globe and a ball with a diameter that is about one-quarter the globe's diameter. Place the globe, which represents the earth, on its stand in the center of a field or playground bathed in early-morning or late-afternoon sunshine. Use scissors and a meterstick or yardstick to cut a piece of string 30 times as long as the globe's (earth's) diameter. For example, if the globe's diameter is 25 cm (10 in), cut the string to 750 cm, or 7.5 m (25 ft) long. Tape one end of the string to the bottom of the globe. Tape the other end to the bottom of the ball that represents the moon. If the globe's diameter is 25 cm (10 in), what should be the approximate diameter of the ball? For the globe you are using, what should be the ball's diameter?

This experiment should be done early in the morning or late in the afternoon when the sun is close to the horizon. If the sun is high in the sky, the moon will have to be in a deep ditch to make a realistic model.

Stand near the globe. Have a partner stretch out the string and move the ball (moon) slowly around the globe (earth) in a counterclockwise direction. But remember, **NEVER LOOK DIRECTLY AT THE SUN!** Where is the ball when it looks like a full moon? Where is the ball when it looks like a crescent moon at sunset? Where is the ball when it looks like a crescent moon at sunrise? Where is the ball when it looks like a half-moon (first quarter) that is seen a week before a full moon? Where is the ball when it looks like a half-moon (third quarter) that is seen a week after a full moon? When the ball is between the globe and the sun, it represents a new moon. But remember, **NEVER LOOK DIRECTLY AT THE SUN!** Shield the sun from your eyes with your hand when you look at this model of a new moon.

Have your partner move the ball (moon) until it lies in the globe's (earth's) shadow. Can you see the earth's curved shadow on the moon? What does the model represent now?

Locate your town or city on the globe. Have your partner place the ball so that it represents a full moon. Turn the globe so that it places your town or city (on the globe) where it would be to see a rising full moon. Turn the globe so that it places your town or city where it would be to see a full moon at midnight. Turn the globe so that it places your town or city where it would be to see a setting full moon. Turn the globe so that it places your town or city where it would be at noon at the time of a full moon.

Repeat the experiment, but this time let your partner stand by the globe while you move the ball (moon) around at the end of the string. Remember, **NEVER LOOK DIRECTLY AT THE SUN!** If you were on the moon, what would the earth look like at the time of a new moon? at the time of first quarter? at the time of a full moon? at the time of third quarter?

> *The moving moon went up the sky,*
> *And nowhere did abide.*
>
> *(Samuel Taylor Coleridge)*

4

A "CLOSER" LOOK AT THE MOON

When Galileo turned the telescope he had made toward the moon in 1610, he opened a new age. Suddenly, his view of the universe changed. And with time, so did the view of all humans. In 1610, all heavenly bodies were believed to be perfectly smooth spheres. But Galileo saw a moon covered with craters and mountains and the shadows cast by both in sunlight.

You can see what Galileo saw. You can share with him a view that shows that the moon is far from smooth. You can see a moon scarred by meteoroids. Most meteoroids that enter the earth's atmosphere burn up. But many meteoroids strike the moon's surface, because the moon has no atmosphere.

DID YOU KNOW. . .?

Galileo's full name was Galileo Galilei. He was born in 1564 and died in 1642. In addition to his discoveries about the moon, he was probably the first to see spots on the sun. He used these spots to show that the sun rotates on its axis every 27 days. He also discovered Jupiter's moons and found that they revolved about that planet. This discovery made it clear that not all bodies revolve about the earth, as most of the world had believed.

Experiment *4.1

THE MOON THROUGH BINOCULARS

To do this experiment you will need:

✔ **binoculars or telescope**

To see the moon as Galileo saw it nearly four hundred years ago, you will need binoculars or a telescope. Focus the binoculars on the moon. You will see a pockmarked surface showing where meteoroids have hit the moon. If you have a telescope, or if you know someone who does, you may be able to see the moon's surface even more clearly.

Try to observe the moon when it is not full. Look at the part of the moon that is close to the line dividing the light part of the moon from the dark part. The shadows there are long. Shadows on the earth are long when the sun is rising or setting. The shadows along the dividing line on the moon are long for the same reason. If you were standing on that dividing line, you would see the sun setting or rising on the moon's horizon.

How do the shadows close to the edge of the dark part of the moon compare with those near the bright edge of the moon? Can you explain why? What do the shadows tell you about the moon's surface?

Continue to look at the moon with binoculars or a telescope. Look at it during all its phases. Watch it as it waxes (gets bigger) from new crescent to first quarter to full. Then watch it as it wanes (gets smaller) from full to third quarter to old crescent.

During the moon's early crescent phase, when it is close to the setting sun, you will see the rest of the moon dimly lighted. This is sometimes called "the new moon with the old moon in its arms." The dim lighting is caused by earthshine. Earthshine is sunlight reflected from the earth to the moon. As the lighted portion of the moon grows bigger and brighter, the dimly lighted portion is less noticeable. This is similar to turning on an outdoor light in the daytime. The light from the bulb is not noticed in bright sunlight.

Look at a full moon through binoculars or a telescope. How do shadows near the center of the moon compare with those nearer the edges of the moon?

Watch the moon's surface closely month after month. You will see that it always looks

FIGURE 14

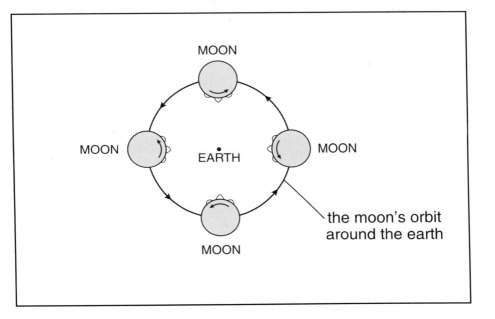

The moon rotates (turns) at the same rate that it revolves about (orbits) the earth. As a result, we always see the same "face" of the moon.

the same. We see only one side of the moon. This means that the moon must rotate (turn) at the same rate that it revolves about (orbits) the earth (see Figure 14). For thousands of years, humans had never seen the far side of the moon. It wasn't until a spaceship launched by the Soviet Union made a loop around the moon and took photographs that we knew what the other side of the moon looked like.

Telescopes

Galileo was able to see the rough surface of the moon by looking through a telescope that he had made. You can make a simple telescope of your own. To do so, you will need to use lenses. One lens with which you are probably familiar is often called a magnifying glass or magnifier.

FIGURE 15

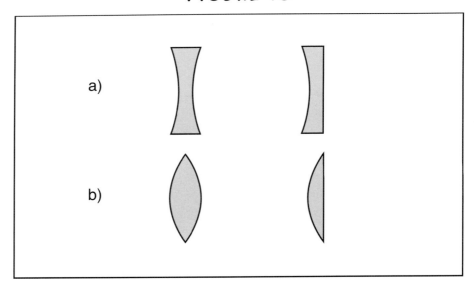

a) Concave lenses are thin in the middle. They may curve inward on one or both sides.

b) Convex lenses are fat in the middle. They may curve outward on one or both sides.

Before you try to make a telescope, it's a good idea to understand lenses. There are two kinds of lenses—convex and concave—as shown in Figure 15. Both lenses work because they can refract (bend) light. In Experiment 4.2, you will examine two or more convex (fatter in the middle) lenses. You might also like to look at concave (thinner in the middle) lenses, but the ones you'll be using to make a telescope will be convex.

DID YOU KNOW. . .?

Two types of telescopes are used by astronomers—refracting and reflecting. Refracting telescopes are those that use lenses to refract light. Reflecting telescopes use convex mirrors to reflect light. The largest refracting telescope is at the Yerkes Observatory near Chicago. Its objective lens is 102 cm in diameter. The size of refracting lenses is limited by their weight. They can become so heavy that they sag, causing the curvature of the lens to change.

Experiment *4.2

CONVEX LENSES, IMAGES, AND FOCAL LENGTHS

To do this experiment you will need:

- ✔ glass cylinder (jar) of water with a lid
- ✔ sunlight
- ✔ 2 sheets of cardboard
- ✔ round balloon
- ✔ twistie
- ✔ 2 convex lenses (magnifiers), one with focal length of 5–10 cm (2–4 in), one with focal length of 10–30 cm (4–12 in)
- ✔ room with window
- ✔ ruler
- ✔ 2 file cards
- ✔ study lamp with a frosted bulb
- ✔ a partner

To see how a convex shape can bend light, hold a closed jar of water in sunlight, as shown in Figure 16a. **NEVER LOOK DIRECTLY AT THE SUN!** Have a partner hold a sheet of cardboard behind the jar (on the opposite side from the sun). Move the jar toward and away from the cardboard until you see a bright line of light on the cardboard. Cover the jar with your hand. What happens to the line of light?

FIGURE 16

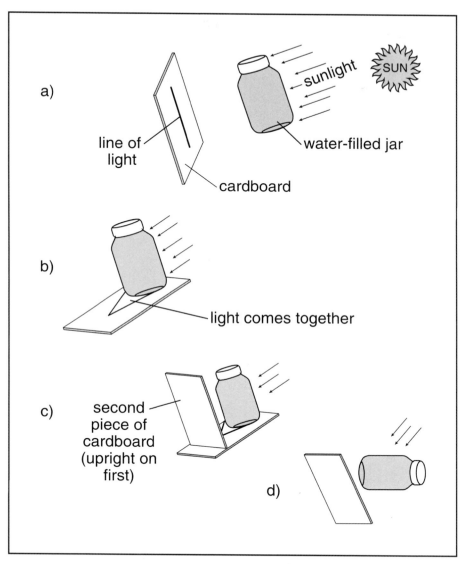

a) Use a water-filled jar to bend light together.

b) Use the cardboard to view the bent light in another way.

c) This method shows both views of light being bent.

d) Is light still bent together when the jar is turned 90 degrees?

How does this experiment show you that the jar of water is bending sunlight?

To see the bending in another way, stand the jar on the end of the cardboard sheet nearest the sun. Tip both jar and cardboard until you can see some of the light that has passed through the jar on the cardboard (see Figure 16b). Notice how the light comes together. This is the lower end of the line of light that you saw before. Place a second sheet of cardboard upright at the point where you see the light come together on the cardboard (see Figure 16c). You can now see the entire line of light.

Rotate the jar through one-quarter turn and again move it toward and away from the cardboard, as shown in Figure 16d. How is the line of light you see now different than the one you saw before? Can you explain the difference? Suppose the container were curved in all directions—a water-filled ball instead of a jar. How do you think it would bend the sunlight?

To see if you are right, attach a round balloon to a water faucet. Fill it with water and seal its neck with a twistie. As you can see, the balloon is shaped like a ball. It is curved in all directions. Hold the balloon in sunlight in front of a sheet of cardboard. Move the balloon

FIGURE 17

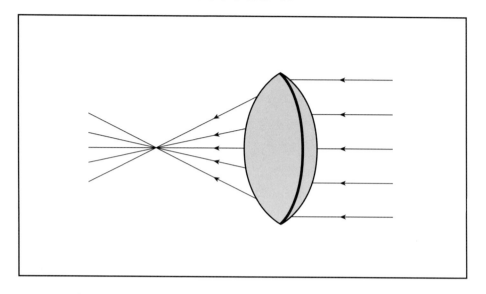

The surface of a convex lens is shaped like a sphere (ball). It bends light together.

toward and away from the cardboard until you can see how the sunlight is bent by the ball of water. Does it bend the light to form a line or a small spot of light? Can you explain why?

A convex lens is curved like part of a sphere (ball), as shown in Figure 17. Therefore, it will bend light coming from all directions inward. **NEVER LOOK AT THE SUN THROUGH A LENS. IT IS EVEN MORE DANGEROUS THAN LOOKING AT THE SUN THROUGH THE LENS IN YOUR OWN EYE!**

Hold a convex lens in sunlight. Have your partner hold a sheet of cardboard behind the lens. Since the surfaces of the lens have the curvature of a sphere, what do you expect to see on the cardboard? Move the lens toward and away from the cardboard so that the light passing through the lens comes together on the cardboard. Were you right?

Convex Lens as Magnifier

Place a convex lens on this page. Look at the print through the lens. Slowly lift the lens. What happens to the apparent size of the letters you see through the lens? Do you see why a convex lens is sometimes called a magnifier?

What happens as you move the lens farther from the print? At some point, can you see the print upside down?

Convex Lens as Image Maker

Convex lenses are used in cameras. To see why, stand on the side of a room opposite a window. Through the window, you should be able to see some distant objects such as trees, mountains, or buildings. Turn the convex lens toward the window. Have your partner hold a sheet of cardboard behind the lens, as shown in Figure 18. Move the lens

FIGURE *18*

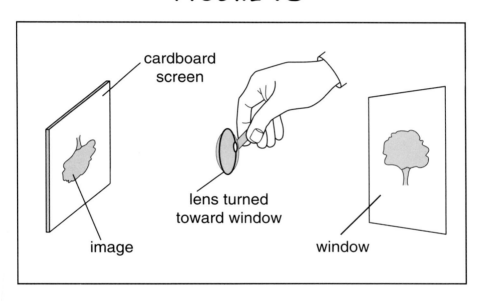

cardboard
screen

lens turned
toward window

image

window

With a convex lens, you can "capture" images on a screen.

toward and away from the cardboard. You will find that you can "capture" the images you see through the window on the cardboard. In a camera, the image would fall on film. Are the images right side up or upside down? Can you see these same images by moving the lens toward and away from your eye?

The images of distant objects (such as the moon) made by using a convex lens are called real images. They are called real images because they can be seen on a screen, like a sheet of cardboard. The magnified right-side-up image of print that you saw before was made by holding the lens close to the print. These magnified right-side-up images that cannot be captured on a screen are called virtual images.

A convex lens can bend light from distant objects back together to form images, as shown in Figure 19. The distance between the lens and the point where light from a very distant object meets to form an image is called the focal length. Every convex lens has a focal length.

Measuring Focal Lengths of Lenses

You can measure the approximate focal length of your lenses quite easily. Stand on the side of a room opposite a window, as you did before. Have a partner hold

FIGURE 19

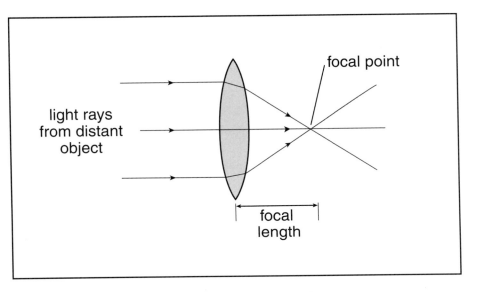

Light from a distant object is brought together by a convex lens. The focal length of the lens is the distance between the lens and the point where the light rays come together (focal point).

a lens while you hold a sheet of cardboard behind it. Your partner can then move the lens until a clear image of the outdoor objects is seen on the cardboard. Use a ruler to measure the distance between the lens and the image on the cardboard. That distance is the approximate focal length of the lens. What is the focal length of each lens?

After dark, if the moon is visible, use each lens to produce an image of the moon. Again measure the distance between the lens and the image to find the focal length. Do this for both lenses. Do these measurements of focal lengths agree closely with the ones you found before?

Place each lens on a card that has the lens's focal length written on it. You will need these lenses in the next experiment.

If you have other convex lenses, find their approximate focal lengths. How is the focal length of a lens related to its convexity (roundness)?

DID YOU KNOW. . . ?

Microscopes are similar to refracting telescopes because both use convex lenses to form enlarged images of the objects observed. In microscopes, a lens with a very short focal length (the objective) is placed near the slide that contains the material being observed. You look through another lens (the eyepiece) with a longer focal length to magnify the image formed by the objective lens.

Experiment *4.3

A Simple Telescope

To do this experiment you will need:

- ✔ at least 2 convex lenses, one with a focal length of 5–10 cm (2–4 in) and one with a focal length of 10–30 cm (4–12 in)
- ✔ tape
- ✔ clay
- ✔ long, thin stick
- ✔ thin paper, such as tissue paper
- ✔ a partner
- ✔ an ADULT

You can use two lenses from Experiment 4.2 to make a telescope. The lens with the longer focal length should be closer to the object being viewed. It is called the objective lens. Its focal length should be at least twice the focal length of the other lens, and it should be as wide as possible. The wider the lens, the more light it will bring together to form an image.

The second lens, the one with the shorter focal length, is called the eyepiece. It is called the eyepiece because it is the lens closer to)ur eye.

Mount the objective lens at one end of a thin stick, as shown in Figure 20a. If the lens has a handle, you can tape it to the end of the stick. If it has no handle, use clay to fix it to the top of the end of the stick. Use this lens to make an image of some distant object (**NOT THE SUN**) as seen through the window you used before. Use a piece of thin paper, such as tissue paper, to capture the real image. The image should be at the lens's approximate focal length, which you know from Experiment 4.2. Use the second lens (eyepiece) to look at the image on the paper (see Figure 20b). Hold the lens near your eye and use it as a magnifier. While you are looking at the magnified image, have your partner remove the paper. You will now be looking directly at the real image formed by the objective lens. Do you expect the image to be right side up or upside down? Were you right?

Mark the point on the stick where the eyepiece is now located. **ASK AN ADULT** to break or cut the stick a short distance beyond the eyepiece. **COVER THE END OF THE STICK WITH TAPE.** The tape will prevent any viewers from getting scratched. Again, adjust the eyepiece for a clear, magnified view of the distant object. Fix the eyepiece to the stick with a small lump of clay, as shown in

FIGURE 20

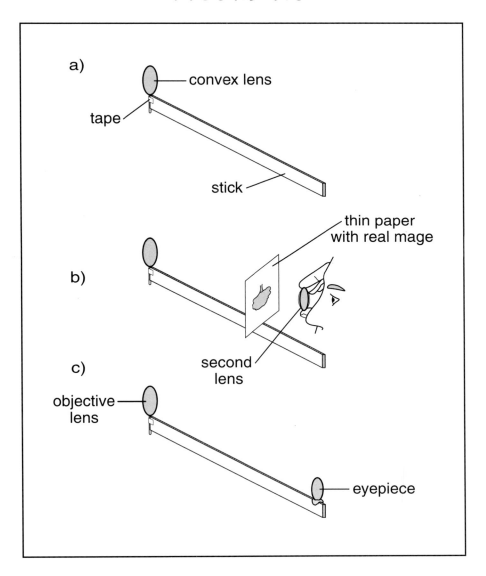

a) Mount a convex lens on one end of a thin stick.

b) Examine an image formed by the lens with a second lens that has a shorter focal length.

c) Mount the second lens on the stick, and you will have made a simple telescope.

Figure 20c. You have made a simple two-lens telescope!

Turn the telescope around so that you are looking through the objective lens. How does this affect the magnification? How does it affect the amount you see through the telescope?

You can estimate the magnification of your telescope. Look through the lenses at a distant object outside the window. Open both eyes. Compare the width or height of some part of the image with the same width or height of the actual object as seen by your eye alone. What is the approximate magnification of your telescope?

Look at the moon through the telescope you have made. How does the image of the moon you see through your telescope compare with the one you see through binoculars?

If possible, try several different lenses for objectives and eyepieces. Which combination gives the greatest magnification?

Experiment *4.4

A BETTER TELESCOPE

To do this experiment you will need:

- ✔ various convex lenses
- ✔ tape
- ✔ cardboard tubes
- ✔ thin cardboard
- ✔ reference sources

To make an easier-to-use telescope, mount the lenses on the ends of cardboard tubes, as shown in Figure 21. One tube should be free to slide back and forth within the other. You can then easily adjust the lenses to obtain clear, magnified images. You can use your telescope to investigate the following questions.

❨ *Why do the telescopes that you can buy have the lenses mounted in tubes?*

❨ *Why are astronomers usually not concerned by the fact that the images seen through a telescope are upside down?*

❨ *How can you build a telescope so that the images you see are right side up?*

FIGURE *21*

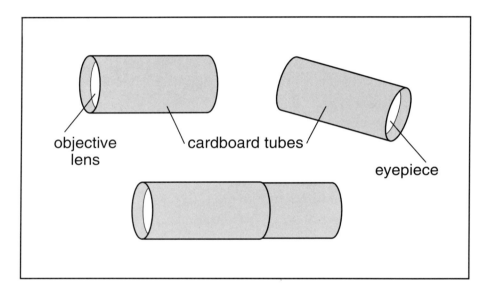

objective lens   cardboard tubes   eyepiece

To make an easier-to-use telescope, mount the lenses in cardboard tubes. Slide one tube into the other to make it easy to adjust the telescope for the best viewing possible.

❰ *How is the focal length of the objective lens divided by the focal length of the eyepiece related to the telescope's magnifying power? (Use a thin sheet of cardboard to measure the focal lengths of the lenses as you did in Experiment 4.2.)*

❰ *You may have noticed that the images you see through your telescope have a rainbowlike ring around them. This is caused by what is known as chromatic aberration, which literally means "the wandering of colors." What can be done to get rid of chromatic aberration? Carry out your own investigation to find out.*

If possible, look at the moon through a commercial refracting telescope. What can you see about the moon that you could not see before?

DID YOU KNOW. . .?

The largest reflecting telescope is found at the W. M. Keck Observatory on Mauna Kea, a mountain on the island of Hawaii. It was built in 1992. Its main mirror has a diameter of 10 meters.

Experiment *4.5

A REFLECTING TELESCOPE

To do this experiment you will need:

- ✔ shaving or makeup mirror
- ✔ sheet of cardboard
- ✔ outdoor objects seen through a window
- ✔ ruler
- ✔ small flat (plane) mirror
- ✔ several convex lenses with different focal lengths
- ✔ commercial reflecting telescope (optional)
- ✔ a partner

When Galileo looked at the moon, he used a telescope with lenses (a refracting telescope). Sir Isaac Newton used a different kind of telescope—a reflecting telescope—to look at the moon. Newton's telescope had a curved (concave) mirror to make a real image of the moon. A side view of a concave mirror is shown in Figure 22. A concave mirror can produce a real image by reflecting light.

You can make a simple reflecting telescope by using a shaving or makeup mirror. The reflecting surface of these mirrors is concave. Put your face close to the concave mirror. You

FIGURE 22

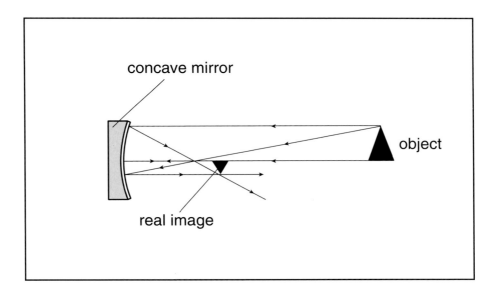

A concave mirror can form real images by reflecting light. Light from the top of the object comes together to form the bottom of the image.

FIGURE 23

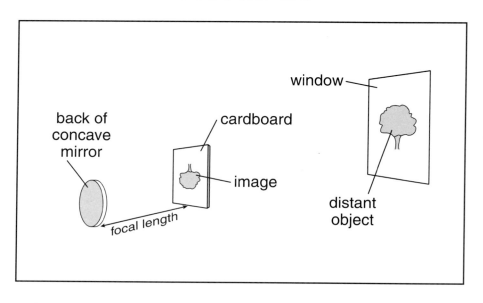

The focal length of a concave mirror can be found easily.

will see a magnified image of your face. But, like a convex lens, it will form real images of distant objects. And, like a convex lens, it has a focal length that can be measured.

To find its focal length, stand on the side of a room opposite a window, as you did before. Have a partner hold the mirror while you hold a sheet of cardboard in front of it (see Figure 23). Move the cardboard until you see a clear image of the outdoor objects on it. Is the image right side up or upside down? How do you know the image is a real image?

Use a ruler to measure the distance between the mirror and the image on the cardboard. That distance is the approximate focal length of the concave mirror. What is the approximate focal length of the mirror you are using?

Most reflecting telescopes, like the one Newton made, use a small flat (plane) mirror to reflect light to the outside of the telescope. In this way, the images can be seen and magnified by looking at them through a lens (see Figure 24). You can do the same thing. Hold a small plane (flat) mirror slightly less than one focal length in front of the concave mirror. Turn the mirror so that you see light reflected from the concave mirror onto the small plane mirror. Then use a convex lens to

FIGURE **24**

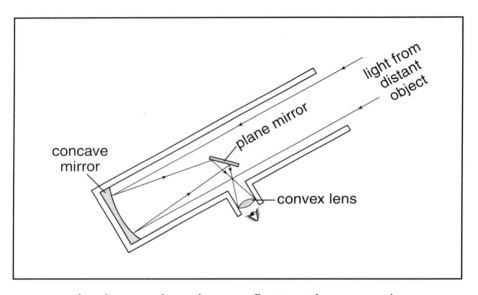

This diagram shows how a reflecting telescope works.

view the image you see in the mirror. Move the lens back and forth until you have a clear image. Does the convex lens magnify the image you saw in the mirror?

Look at the image using lenses with different focal lengths. How does the focal length affect the magnification of the image you see?

Use the reflecting telescope you have made to look at the moon. What is the approximate magnifying power of your reflecting telescope?

If possible, look at the moon through a commercial reflecting telescope. What can you see about the moon that you could not see before?

DID YOU KNOW. . .?

Earth is not the only planet with a moon. Jupiter has twelve moons, Saturn has nine, Uranus has five, and Neptune and Mars each have two. Only Mercury, Venus, and Pluto appear to have no natural satellites.

I with borrow'd silver shine,
What you see is none of mine.
(Jonathan Swift)

<u>5</u>

MORE ABOUT THE MOON

The moon is the only celestial body of which we have firsthand knowledge. We have such knowledge because during a three-and-a-half-year period between 1969 and 1972, humans walked on the moon. But we knew a lot about the moon and its effects on the earth long before we landed on it. Still, sending men safely to the moon and back was truly an amazing feat. Much was learned about the moon by this direct contact and from the 381 kg (840 lbs) of moon rocks that astronauts brought back to the earth.

The Moon's Origin

 Where did the moon come from? No one knows for sure. But a number of explanations were proposed well before men landed on the lunar surface. One is the fission theory. It holds that when the solar system was forming, the moon was part of the earth. At that time—about 5 billion years ago—the earth was spinning very fast. As it spun, it became disk-shaped and about one fiftieth of it broke off and became the moon.

Another explanation is that both the earth and the moon were formed side by side at about the same time. The solar system, it is believed, once consisted of a spinning disk of tiny particles. At the center of the disk, where the particles were very concentrated, the sun formed. Farther out, the force of gravity gradually pulled particles together around the larger particles. The larger particles were the nuclei on which the planets and their moons grew to their present sizes. In the case of the moon and the earth, they grew side by side. But the earth became much bigger than the moon. As a result, the moon circled the earth while they both circled the sun.

A third theory holds that the moon was moving like a giant meteoroid through space. It came close to the earth at a speed that allowed the earth's gravity to "capture" it. This caused the moon to orbit the earth as the earth orbits the sun.

Still another explanation is that the young earth was struck by a giant meteoroid. The impact was so great that it sent vast amounts of rocks and dust flying off into space. With time, gravity pulled these particles together to form the moon. A similar theory holds that the earth was hit by many smaller meteoroids. The bombardment produced so much heat that matter boiled off the earth and then condensed into rocks. These rocks were then pulled together by gravity to form the moon.

The origin of the moon remains a mystery. All the theories of its origin have flaws. Regardless of its origin, the moon will continue to orbit the earth for millennia to come. But each year, the moon moves about 2 cm (1 in) farther away from us. Even as the earth and the moon slowly separate, they continue to pull on one another. The moon's pull on the earth creates the tides so familiar to those who live by an ocean.

The Moon and Tides

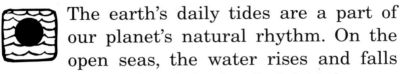 The earth's daily tides are a part of our planet's natural rhythm. On the open seas, the water rises and falls about 75 cm (30 in). Its height changes considerably more along coastal areas. In the Bay of Fundy, between Nova Scotia and New Brunswick, tides cause the water to rise and fall by as much as 21 m (70 ft).

It is the moon's gravity that pulls on the earth and creates the tides (see Figure 25). The sun is also partly responsible for the tides, but its effect is less than the moon's. Even the solid part of the earth is pulled about 11.5 cm (4.5 in) toward the moon during high tide.

The friction created along the earth's surface by the tides is slowing the earth's rotation by about 0.02 sec per century. The effect is not noticeable over a lifetime, but there has been a large change over the earth's long history. Certain shelled creatures that live in the sea form daily and monthly bands on their shells. Fossil forms of these organisms show us that 400 million years ago a day was about 22 hours long. Other evidence shows that 4.5 billion years ago a day was only 5–6 hours long, and the moon orbited the earth in a time equal to what we now call a week.

FIGURE 25

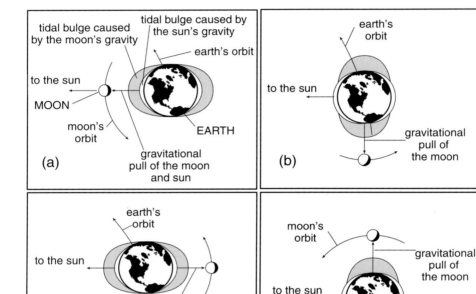

(a) tidal bulge caused by the moon's gravity / tidal bulge caused by the sun's gravity / earth's orbit / to the sun / MOON / moon's orbit / EARTH / gravitational pull of the moon and sun

(b) earth's orbit / to the sun / gravitational pull of the moon

(c) earth's orbit / to the sun / moon's orbit / gravitational pull of the moon

(d) moon's orbit / gravitational pull of the moon / to the sun

The earth's tides are caused by the moon's and the sun's gravity. This is most obvious at:

a) new moon and spring tide;   b) first quarter and neap tide;

c) full moon and spring tide;   d) third quarter and neap tide

The tidal bulges occur on opposite sides of the earth. The bulge nearest the moon is caused by the moon's gravity. The bulge on the opposite side (farthest from the moon) is caused by a centrifugal effect of the earth's spin. The tidal bulge caused by the sun is less than half that caused by the moon. Tides are also affected by the moon's distance from the earth. Tides at the moon's perigee are higher than those when the moon is at apogee.

When the moon, earth, and sun are along a roughly straight line (new moon and full moon), the tides are called spring tides. Spring tides are higher than neap tides, which occur when the moon is at first and third quarter.

Man in the Moon

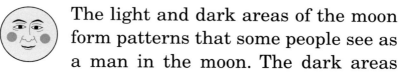 The light and dark areas of the moon form patterns that some people see as a man in the moon. The dark areas (maria) may be seen as the eyes, nose, and mouth set in a giant round face. Others see in these areas the head, body, arms, and legs of a figure. Still others see the shape of a rabbit. Do you see a face, figure, rabbit, or something else when you look at a full moon?

Of course, the man in the moon is imaginary. No one lives on the moon because there is no air on the moon. However, we know that people have lived there for short periods of time. Between 1969 and 1972, twelve United States astronauts walked on the moon's surface. But they had to bring canisters of compressed air with them. Someday, people may live on the moon for long periods of time. But they will have to bring or manufacture their own air.

Man on the Moon

 Before men first walked on the moon in 1969, there was a good bit of exploration. In 1959, instruments on board the Soviet Union's *Luna 2* showed there was no magnetic field on the moon. This information was transmitted to the earth before the spacecraft crashed into the lunar surface. During the same year, the Soviet Union's *Luna 3* orbited the moon and took photographs of its back side. It was this spacecraft that first revealed to the world that the back side of the moon has no maria (dark areas).

In 1965, the United States *Ranger* probes provided close-up views of the moon's surface. In 1966, the Soviet spacecraft *Luna 9* made the first successful soft landing on the moon. This landing made it clear that the moon was not covered with a thick layer of dust, as some scientists had believed.

From 1966 to 1968, probes that were part of the United States Surveyor program photographed the lunar surface and carried out soil analyses. During the same period, the United States Lunar Orbiter program was providing a series of detailed photographs that allowed NASA scientists to draw maps of the moon's surface.

Apollo 8 and *Apollo 10* were two manned flights by United States astronauts to orbit the moon. The flight of *Apollo 11* then sent a Lunar Landing Module to a soft landing on the surface of the moon on July 20, 1969. Following the landing, astronaut Neil Armstrong could be heard to say, "Tranquility Base here. The *Eagle* has landed." A few hours later, Armstrong became the first human to walk on the moon. As his foot touched the lunar surface, he said, "That's one small step for a man, one giant leap for mankind."

Altogether, *Apollo* spacecraft made six landings on the moon. In each landing, two men walked on the moon. A third crew member remained in a command module that stayed in orbit around the moon until rejoined by the Lunar Landing Module. Table 2 shows *Apollo* missions that made trips to the moon.

The rocks that astronauts brought back to the earth were tested to see how old they were. The age of rocks can be determined by measuring the amount of radioactive uranium and lead in them. Rocks from the lowlands (maria) were found to be about 3.1–3.8 billion years old. The lighter highland rocks were 4–4.6 billion years old. The different ages of the rocks helped to confirm the belief that meteoroids broke through the crust on the

TABLE 2

APOLLO MISSIONS TO THE MOON

Mission	Launch Date	Lunar Landing Date	Crew	Accomplishment
Apollo 8	Dec. 21, 1968	Never landed	Frank Borman James A. Lovell, Jr. William A. Anders	First manned mission to orbit the moon
Apollo 10	May 18, 1969	Never landed	Thomas Stafford John Young Eugene Cernan	Moved lunar module within 3.5 km (2.2 mi) of the moon
Apollo 11	July 16, 1969	July 20, 1969	Neil A. Armstrong Michael Collins Edwin E. Aldrin, Jr.	First manned landing on the moon Armstrong and Aldrin walk on the moon at *Mare Tranquillitatis*
Apollo 12	Nov. 14, 1969	Nov. 19, 1969	Charles Conrad, Jr. Richard Gordon, Jr. Alan L. Bean	Second manned landing, this time at *Oceanus Procellarum*
Apollo 13	April 11, 1970	Never landed	James Lovell, Jr. John Swigert, Jr. Fred Haise, Jr.	Accident on board forced spaceship to return after going around back side of the moon
Apollo 14	Jan. 31, 1971	Feb. 5, 1971	Alan Shepard Stuart Roosa Edgar Mitchell	Landed on *Fra Mauro*
Apollo 15	July 26, 1971	July 30, 1971	David Scott Alfred Worden James Irwin	Landed near Apennine Mountains
Apollo 16	April 16, 1972	April 20, 1972	John Young Thomas Mattingly II Charles Duke	Landed near Crater Descartes
Apollo 17	Dec. 7, 1972	Dec. 11, 1972	Eugene Cernan Ronald Evans Harrison Schmitt	Landed in Tautus Littrow

near side of the moon about 3.5 billion years ago. The breaks allowed the molten rock below the surface to well up and flood the lowlands.

Much was learned about the moon by the astronauts who walked on its surface. In addition to their experiments and the rocks they brought back, they left a number of instruments that continued to relay information to the earth long after they had left. For example, instruments that record vibrations caused by meteoroids showed that 80 to 150 meteoroids strike the moon each year. The size of these space rocks varies from 1 to 1,000 kg (2 lbs to a ton).

Will humans ever return to the moon? Many people think we should. There are valuable minerals on the moon that could be mined and used to manufacture the goods on which we all depend. As the earth's minerals become depleted, we may turn to the moon. In fact, there are plans to build space colonies on orbiting modules near the moon. These colonies, where some of the earth's excess population could live, would make use of the materials extracted from the moon. So human trips to the moon may not have ended. Perhaps you will someday walk on the moon or live in a home that orbits our only natural satellite.

☆ FURTHER READING ☆

Adler, David. *All About the Moon.* Mahwah, N.J.: Troll Communications, 1983.

Asimov, Isaac. *Why Does the Moon Change Shape?* Milwaukee, Wis.: Gareth Stevens, Inc., 1991.

Baker, David. *Living on the Moon.* Vero Beach, Fla.: Rourke Corp., 1989.

Estalella, Robert. *Our Satellite: The Moon.* Hauppauge, N.Y.: Barron's Educational Series, Inc., 1994.

Gardner, Robert. *Projects in Space Science.* New York: Messner, 1988.

———. *Space: Frontier of the Future.* New York: Doubleday, 1980.

———. *Yesterday's Science, Today's Technology: Space.* New York: Twenty-First Century Books, Inc., 1994.

Gardner, Robert and Dennis Shortelle. *The Future and the Past.* New York: Messner, 1989.

George, Michael. *The Moon.* Plymouth, Minn.: Child's World, Inc., 1992.

Santrey, Laurence. *Moon*. Mahwah, N.J.: Troll Communications, 1985.

Simon, Seymour. *The Moon*. Old Tappan, N.J.: Four Winds Press, 1984.

Sneider, Cary I. *Earth, Moon & Stars*. Berkeley, Calif.: Lawrence Hall of Science, 1986.

Sorensen, Lynda. *Moon*. Vero Beach, Fla.: Rourke Corp., 1993.

Sullivan, George. *The Day We Walked on the Moon*. New York: Scholastic, Inc., 1990.

✰ LIST OF MATERIALS ✰

A
almanac

B
balloon
battery, D-cell
binoculars or telescope

C
calendar
cardboard sheets
chalk
clay
clock
compass, magnetic
convex lenses

D
dark room

F
file card

G
globe

J
jars

L
lamp
lightbulb

M
meterstick (yardstick)
mirror, makeup
moon

N
newspaper, daily
notebook

O
open field

R
room with window
ruler

S
scissors
stick
string
Styrofoam ball
sunlight

T
tape
tissue paper
toothpicks
twistie

W
watch
wire stripper
wire, insulated copper

☆ INDEX ☆

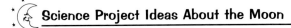